Advance Guide to Dominate Binary Options

Jordon Skyes

copyright page

CONTENTS

	Introduction	v
1	Chapter 1 Advanced Strategies of Binary Options	1
2	Chapter 2 The Gamma Scalping Strategy for Expert Binary Traders	12
3	Chapter 3 The Pivot Bear Trading Strategy	14
4	Chapter 4 Using Channel Identification in Binary Options	18
5	Chapter 5 Binary Options Fence Trading Strategy	23
6	Chapter 6 Fibonacci in Binary Options Trading	25
	Chapter 7 Straddle Strategy	27
	Chapter 8 Draw Down Strategy	29
	Chapter 9 Collar Strategy Protective Options	32
	Chapter 10 Protective Put Strategy	34
	Chapter 11 Covered Call Strategy	37
	Chapter 12 A Great Binary Options Strategy-Long Box Trading	39
	Chapter 13 Money Management-Stop Loss and Profit Taking	41
	Chapter 14 Risk and Bet Size-Hedging and Stop Loss	43
	Chapter 15 Scalping: Binary Options Strategies	46
	Chapter 16 The Forex Multiple Time Frames Strategy with Binary Options	48
	Chapter 17 Identifying Trend Reversals	50
	Conclusion	53

INTRODUCTION

What are Binary Options?

Known by various other names such as "Digital Options" or "All or Nothing Options", binary options trading is a new alternative way of investing in options. It had gained tremendous popularity during the last few years. Its popularity is largely due to the fact that binary options are very simple to trade with. Unlike traditional options, traders of binary options only need to predict the direction of the option's underlying asset price in order to profit from their investment. Furthermore, the returns of binary options are predetermined allowing traders to quantify their investment risk.

Binary Options History

Binary options were a recent introduction in the financial markets. It made to debut into the mainstream financial world in when the Options Clearing Corporation proposed to the SEC to allow binary options to be traded in the mainstream markets. Hence, following a rule change, the American stock exchange and CBOE began to publicly offer binary options to the markets in 2008. Initially, binary options trading were just limited to contracts on the S&P 500 and CBOE Volatility Index. However as the market matured, more and more binary options contracts were offered to be traded covering a diverse range of underlying assets.

Why Trade in Binary Options?

Book smallBecause of the unique characteristics of binary options, they represent an excellent way to invest in the complex and confusing financial markets. As there are only two possible outcomes for binary options, in-the-money or out-of-the-money, traders don't have to worry about the unlimited risk factor that they faced trading with traditional options.

Returns are known beforehand and there is a wide choice of assets available for the trader's investment consideration. And because binary options contracts cover the four (4) main financial markets, trading is available 24/6. In the event of a trade being unsuccessful, some binary options brokers also offer a refund up to 15% of invested capital to traders. With high payouts, easy access to the markets and the availability of trading regardless of the time of day, it is no wonder that the binary options market is attracting so many "greenhorns" to invest in the financial markets.

When to Trade Binary Options?

CalendarDespite claims to the contrary by same unscrupulous brokers, you should only start trading in binary options once you have grasped the basics of fundamental and technical analysis. You also have to ensure that you have sufficient prior planning before jumping into the water.

As binary options are quick expiring options, this usually leaves you very little time to contemplate on the best time to enter the market. Nevertheless, there are some strategies that you can follow to assist you in deciding when the best times to trade in a binary option are:

- Trade Based On Important Economic News
- Trade When The Major Markets Are Opened
- Trade According To The Trend
- How to Trade in Binary options?
- One, two, three, Trade!

With the technological advancement in the World Wide Web in recent years, it is now relatively simple for you to start trading in binary options.

The first thing that you need to do is to find a reliable binary options broker and open a trading account.

After opening a trading account, select an asset that is creating excitement in the market. (This should be based on the techniques that we will discuss later in this guide.)

Once you have decided on what asset to trade in, select the time-frame that you want to trade in.

Decide on the amount that you want to invest in.

Once you have gone through the above steps, just sit back and wait to see if your trade expires in-the-money or if you made a loss.

CHAPTER 1 ADVANCED STRATEGIES OF BINARY OPTIONS

MACD & Bollinger Bands Binary Trading Strategy

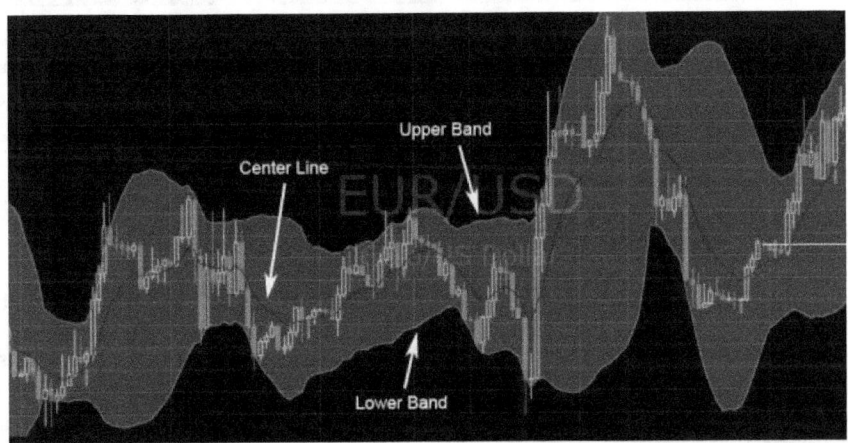

This strategy is an expansion of the MACD trading strategy. While the MACD is used for identifying the prevailing trend, this strategy adds the Bollinger bands as an additional indicator for a trade trigger in order to minimize the likelihood of a false signal. Although the MACD indicator is reasonably reliable, it is not without its shortcomings. One of its shortcomings is the fact that a wild price swing can result in prices varying significantly for the market trend. Another shortcoming of the MACD is because the indicator is a lagging indicator. And because of this lag, the MACD is susceptible to false signals as signals are generated only after prices have bottomed out or peaked.

The Bollinger Bands

A creation of by a technical analyst by the John Bollinger, Bollinger Bands comprises of an exponential moving average acting as a center line flanked by two price channels, an upper band, and a lower band. These bands will contract or expand as prices decrease or increase in volatility respectively.

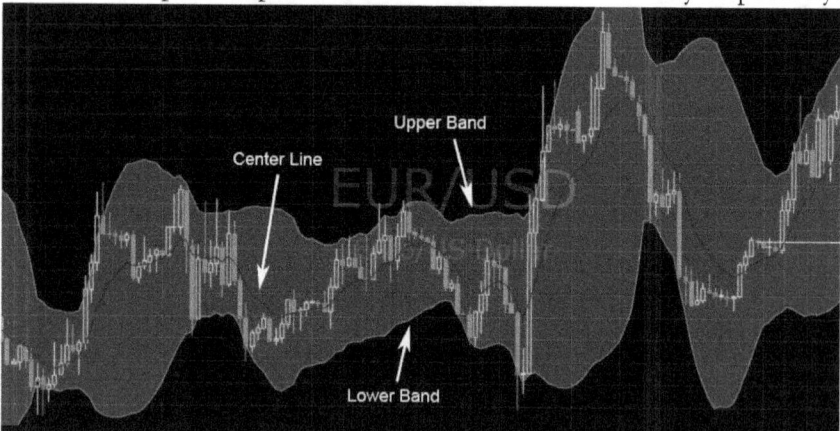

b Analysts use the Bollinger Bands as a mean to help trace how the market is trading by filtering out the price action. Regardless of how prices are fluctuating, analysts are still able to monitor if the trading activities are still confined around the primary trend. Hence by using the Bollinger Bands, traders can hope to cancel out the effects of false signals as a result of wild price swings.

Advantages of the MACD & Bollinger Bands Strategy

There are several advantages of using this double indicators strategy to trade binaries. First of all, the MACD is a fairly dependable indicator for generating trading signals. It is reasonably accurate and simple to use. It allows traders to have an insight into what is happening in the market.

Secondly, the Bollinger Bands is a powerful tool especially for binary trading as it is an enveloping indicator. Regardless of which direction the market is heading towards to, traders can depend on it to trade the market. In addition, it cuts down the risk of false signals.

Lastly, this double indicators strategy is able to provide traders with precise market entry points making it easy to trade dynamic and volatile financial markets. Even though traders generally have difficulties is determining when to exit the market, this strategy is still able to provide them with some indication of where the exit points should be.

Disadvantages of the MACD & Bollinger Bands Strategy

Like all trading strategies, there are always some limitations to them. Likewise, the MACD & Bollinger Bands strategy is no exception. While this strategy is great for trading short term inaries like 60 seconds options, it becomes riskier as we stretch the timeframe of the trade longer.

The Bottom Line

Although the above-mentioned strategy helps to reduce the incidences of false signals, it doesn't entirely eliminate them from cropping up. Further analysis is required if traders wish the chances of acting on false signals.

On the whole, the MACD & Bollinger Bands strategy is quite effective especially when we are dealing with short-term binaries. But still, it is not without its own risks. But this is why we use double indicators as the readings from both indicators are used to confirm each other.

Interpreting the MACD Indicator for Binary Trading

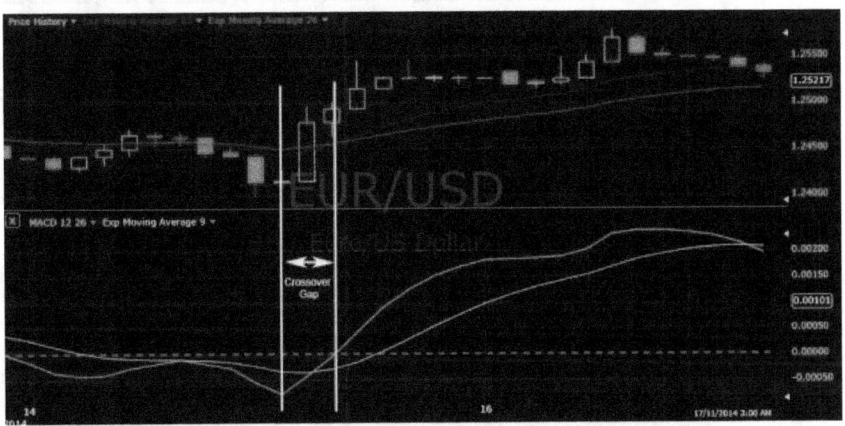

While the concept of binary options trading is a simple matter, to get ahead, a trader must be able to formulate an effective trading strategy on his own. In this article, we will take an in-depth look at how we can use the Moving Average Convergence Divergence (MACD) technical indicator to further our trading advantage when trading Call/Put binaries. Analysts generally use the MACD indicator to help them understand the magnitude of the momentum in the market.

The MACD uses the relationship between a shorter moving average of prices and a longer moving average of prices to discerning the momentum of a trend. It is derived by deducting 26 days exponential moving average (EMA) from 12 days EMA. To act a trigger for a trading signal, a 9 days EMA is then plotted over the MACD.

Interpreting the MACD Indicator for Binary Trading

The diagram below shows an example of what a MACD and the signal line will look like on a candlestick chart.

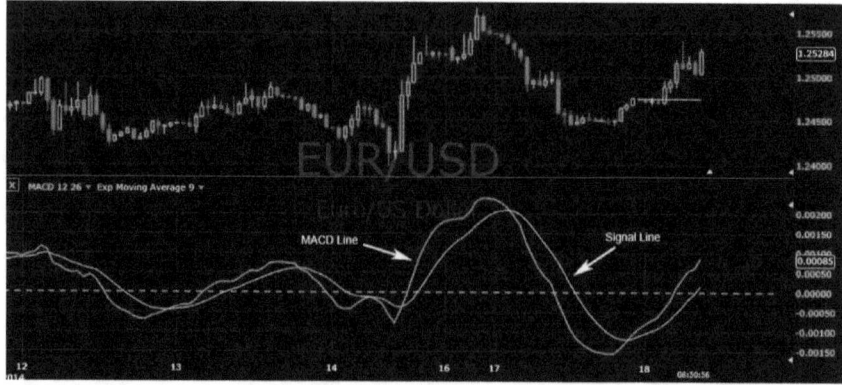

.However, if the MACD is to be of any use, you need to be able to interpret it correctly and know what each signal is supposed to indicate.

Crossovers:

Crossovers between the MACD and the signal line can occur from above or below the signal line. If the crossover is from below the signal line, this is taken as indicative of a bullish signal. On the other hand, if the crossover is from above the signal line, this is taken as a bearish signal

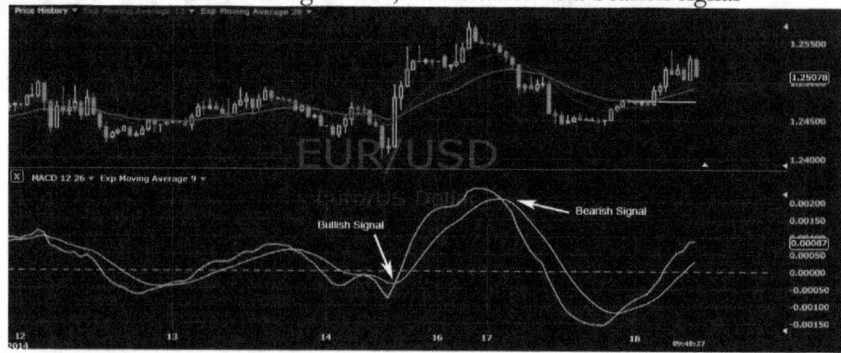

Entry Signal:

With reference to the figure below, since the crossover of the MACD and signal line occurs faster than the crossover of the two EMAs, there will be a slight gap between the two crossovers. You can use this crossover gap as an advance signal for entry into the market.

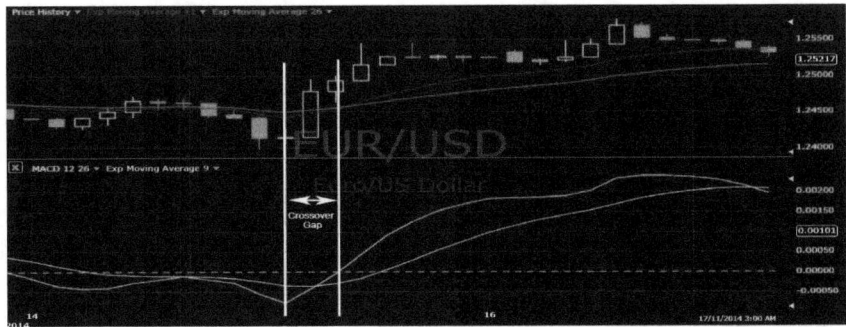

As to whether you should purchase a Call option or a Put option, this will depend on whether the crossover is bullish of bearish. If the signal is bullish, buy Call options immediately after MACD and signal line crossover point. Conversely, if the crossover is bearish, buy Put options right after the crossover point.

While the MACD is an excellent indicator, you must be careful not to put too much emphasis on it. This is because a price shock could easily cause the prices to vary significantly from the prevailing trend. In such a case, it is always prudent to reconfirm your trading signal with another indicator before deciding to act.

CHAPTER 2 THE GAMMA SCALPING STRATEGY FOR EXPERT BINARY TRADERS

The binary options gamma scalping strategy is an advanced trading strategy for experienced binary options traders. Only traders who are extremely knowledgeable and well capitalized should ever consider using the gamma

scalping strategy
Delta & Gamma

Gamma is a Greek term used to describe the rate of change of a financial option's delta as compared to the price of the option's underlying asset. Delta or "hedge ratio" in financial trading refers to the ratio of change of an underlying asset price as compared to the option's price. For an example of an option has a delta of 0.75, this mean for every $1 change in the price of an underlying asset, the price of the option will change by $0.75. So in other words, if an option has a gamma of 0.10, this mean the option will change by 0.10 delta as the price of the underlying asset changes.

Why Gamma Is Important

As an option moves more into the money, the bigger the option's delta will be and the more it moves out of the money, the smaller the option's delta will be. Since the price of an underlying asset is never constant in a dynamic market, this means an option's delta will also be constantly changing. Understanding the changes in the option's delta is crucial for a trader as it can affect the trader's bottom line. Hence, there is a need to keep track of an option's gamma.

The Gamma Scalping Strategy Explained

Basically, the gamma scalping strategy seeks to scalp gains through the adjustment of an option's delta by taking a long gamma position in times of shifting markets. In the financial markets if the volatility of an underlying asset is considered "too cheap", this is taken as meaning that the volatility of that underlying asset is higher than its market price. Under such a situation, it can be profitable for a trader to open an option position and move that position forward in the spot market since all such maneuvers have long gamma positions.

As mentioned earlier, when an underlying asset's price increases, its option's delta also increases. And if a trader has taken out a long option position and had hedged his position, he would also gain a long delta position from the consequent increase in the spot market. It is immaterial if the trader invested in a long put or call position since the option's delta will still increase with an increase in the underlying asset price.

In order to maintain a mean market position, a trader simply just have to buy puts if he wants to add to his position or sell calls to decrease his exposure and vice versa (depending on whether he is facing long deltas or short deltas).

Advantage and Disadvantage

The main advantage of the gamma scalping strategy is the fact that it cancels out the negative effect of time decay (theta) and collapses in the option's Vega. This is due to the fact that all gamma scalping strategies are affected to some extent by changes in liquidity and volatility.

However, the disadvantage of this strategy is the fact that a trader might need to wait for some time before making his anticipated move which will ultimately result in his position losing value due to theta. Nevertheless, trying to buy patience and to offset theta is the whole idea of the gamma scalping strategy.

CHAPTER 3 THE PIVOT BEAR TRADING STRATEGY

Pivot Point Bear strategy is an excellent strategy not only for risk control when trading binary options but also can be used as an indicator or monitoring tool. Traders are advised to familiarize themselves with this strategy so they will provide them with a powerful tool in their arsenal of trading strategies

What Are Pivot Points?

By definition, pivot points are a type of technical indicator that is used by technical analysts to verify the primary market trend over a range of different time frames. It is essentially a point derived from the average of the previous day's high, low and closing price. For technical analysts, pivot points are mostly used for determining the resistance and support levels of a trend. In the analysis of pivot points, technical analysts calculate the first set of support and resistance level by using the asset's price range from the pivot point to either the asset's previous day high or low prices. As for the second set of support and resistance level, it is derived from utilizing the full range of the asset's previous day highs and lows prices.

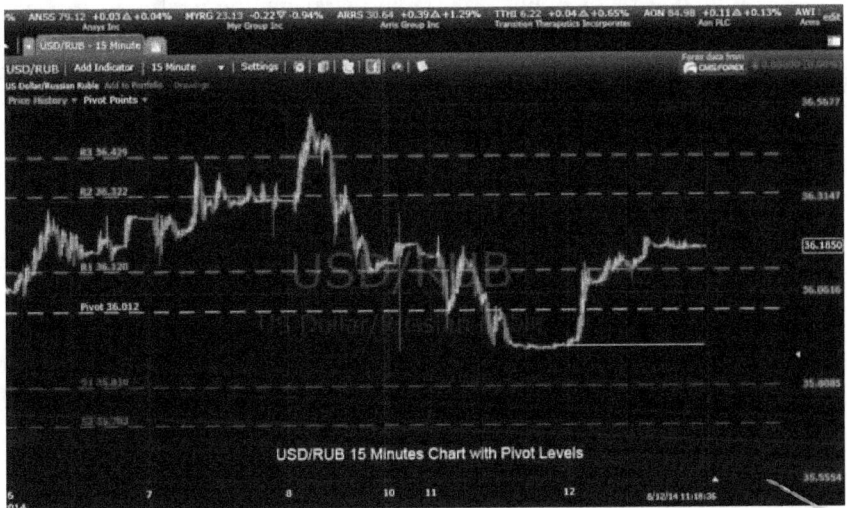

Calculating Pivot Points

There are actually a few ways of calculating pivot points. One method is by the 5 points system as we have mentioned earlier above. With this system, in addition to 2 support and resistance levels, the asset's previous day closing price, its high and low prices (altogether 5 price points) are used to derive point.

Uses of Pivot Points

The pivot points derived can be utilized in 2 ways. Firstly, traders can use it to determine the primary trend in the market. If prices are breaching the pivot point price level in an upward manner, then the market is regarded as being bullish. If however, prices are breaching the pivot point level in a downward manner, then the market is seen as bearish. It should be noted that pivot points are essentially short-term indicators of the market trend. Its validity is only for a single day.

The second use of pivot point levels is an indicator as to when traders should enter or exit the market. For example, if prices are breaching a resistance level, this is the time that the trader should enter the market. On the other hand, if prices are breaching a support level, this mean the trader should get out of the market. A stop loss order can be set at this support level to be triggered if the level is breached.

Pivot Point Bear Trading Strategy

With the pivot point bear trading strategy, the goal is to capitalize on down trending market. To get an indication of the magnitude of prices moving downwards, the trader will use pivot point levels to plot the movement of price changes. With each passing day, the trader will be able to see how low prices are moving to. To confirm the bearish conditions of the market, traders can use the "inverted hammer" candlestick pattern as an indicator. Using the daily pivot point level as a threshold, if the opening price of the opening candlestick is below the threshold, then the trader can be fairly certain that the market is bearish with prices trending downwards for the day. The same principle can also be applied by traders wanting to trade a bullish market.

Regardless of whether one is a new or experienced trader, this trading strategy is simple and easy to apply. With enough practice, traders can easily obtain an accurate indication of the market trend for the trading day.

CHAPTER 4 USING CHANNEL IDENTIFICATION IN BINARY OPTIONS

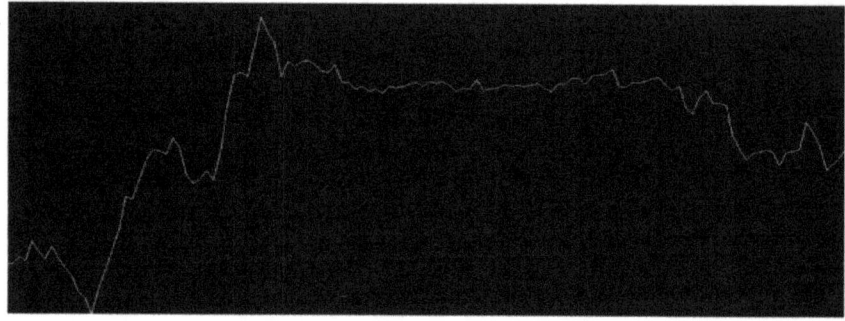

Traders dream about stumbling across an asset trading in a channel. It has all the advantages of trading with the trend, but also provides a bunch of signals which make trading really profitable. Channels are often hard to identify and carry a risk of breaking unexpectedly, which is why they often aren't discussed in many binary options strategies. But when they do appear, they can give the opportunity for substantial profit in a short time, which makes them worthwhile to discuss.

   A channel is basically when the market get's confined between two trendlines. There are several reasons for why the market would behave like this, such as investor risk appetite, Fibonacci levels among others. But that's really advanced and is only useful to someone who spends all day tracking the market.

So how can you identify a channel? Well, this is what one looks like;-

Notice how the market obligingly keeps between the two red lines, and each time it comes up to touch one, it backs off. Channels never last forever, so what you are looking for is to get in a few good trades while it lasts and always keep an eye out for what happened near the end when the channel ended. In this chart, you could have had up to 11 trades between puts and calls that would end up in the money.

As you can see, the principal advantage of a channel over trading a trend is that it gives you signals in both directions —whereas in trend trading you only get signals in one direction. This potentially doubles the number of trades you can make.

Catching a channel

Of course in that picture, it's pretty easy to identify the channel once it has already formed. The idea is to catch it in the beginning stages. To do that, we turn to our handy charting software and open a chart as a line graph. The reason is that the tops and bottoms of movements are easier to identify because a line graph only shows the close for each period. Here's what that chart above looked like as the channel was forming:

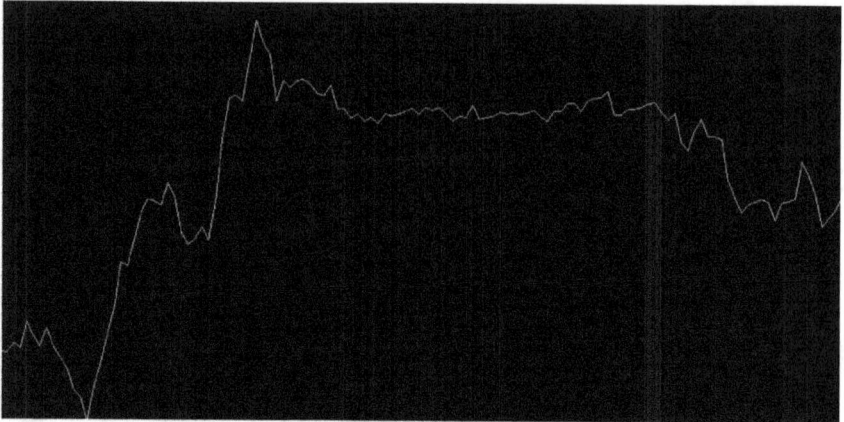

Near the end, it looks like there might be a downtrend forming. A trend, of course, is a great opportunity to trade on its own merits, but if we want to see if the trend is sticking to the channel, we need to find three pivot points.

Pivot points are where the market changes direction, and they are conveniently indicated by the arrows. Any trading software worth its salt will have a channel tool that you can apply to the graph. You want to trace the channel tool over the two points that are on the same side. In this case, they are the two on top like this:

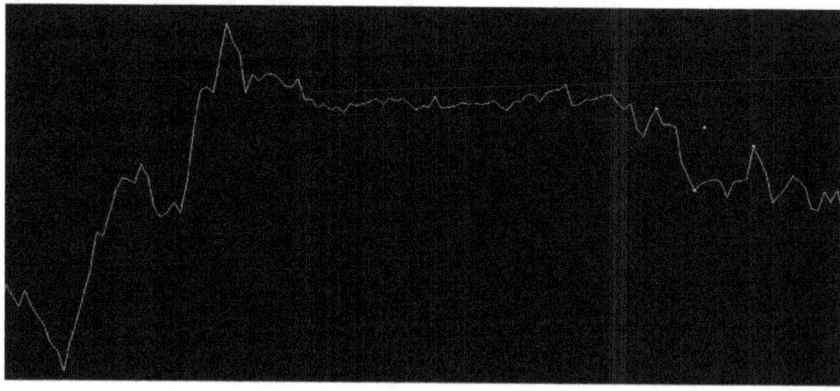

Note how the drawing points are placed on the points of the movements. If your software doesn't have a channel tool, you can draw a channel with two trend lines. Just remember that they have to be parallel, which can be a bit tricky to draw.

Then you want to switch your chart to Japanese candlesticks. You always have to be alert for the possibility that the market will break out of the channel, but in the meantime, you want to watch for when the market comes down to touch one of the sides of the channel. As long as the market stays in the channel that means it the market will move in the opposite direction and is a great opportunity to buy an option

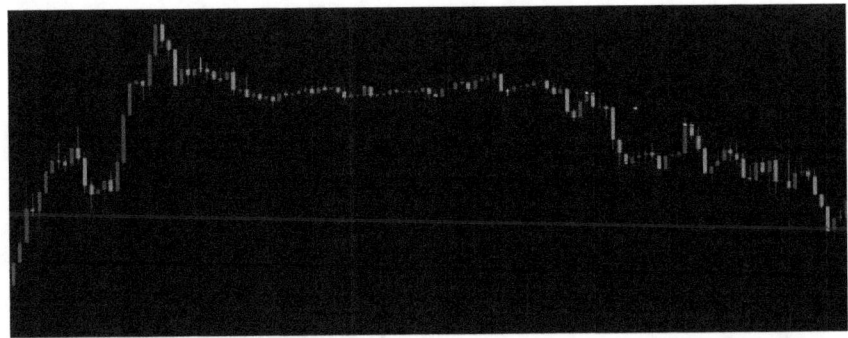

If the market touches the top of the channel, you want to buy a put – expect the market to go down. If the market touches the bottom then you buy a call – expect the market to go up.

Typically you'd set your chart to the same timeframe as the expiry of your options. For example, if the options expire every 15 minutes, then you want to chart in a 15 minute period.

This strategy works in conjunction with other trend strategies, giving you the second set of signals to either confirm the trend or show retracement opportunities.

CHAPTER 5 BINARY OPTIONS FENCE TRADING STRATEGY

The Binary Options Fence Trading Strategy is designed to help traders reduce the risk of investment through the use of binary options. Basically, the strategy requires the purchase of two (2) options contracts on the same asset. This is because the trader needs to cover both sides of the market. Hence, he buys both "Above" and "Below" contracts to "fence" in the prices of the asset in between the strike prices of these two (2) contracts. With this strategy, the trader is able to reduce his investment risk and also profit from the market even without really having to choose which direction the market will go.

For example, an underlying asset is presently trading at $20. He predicts that the price of the asset will rise within the next 10 minutes and thus buys an "Above" contract for $1000 to expire in 30 minutes. Initially, the market moves in favor of the trader until unforeseen events cause prices to fall. If the trader does nothing, the value of his investment will start to decline and ultimately leaves the trader out of the money. But with the fencing strategy, the trader can reverse this undesirable situation and lock in his profit.

Suppose the trader purchase a "Below" contract for $1000 when the price was trading at $25 after dropping from the peak of $38 just a few minutes prior. Assuming the payout is 85%, and the expiration price of the asset is between $20 and $25, the trader will be able to collect on both contracts earning a total profit of $1700 ($850 + $850).

If the expiration price finishes ABOVE $25, then the "Above" contract is in the money while the "Below" contract is out of the money. However, if the expiration price finishes BELOW $25, then the "Above" contract is out the money while the "Below" contract is in of the money. In either case, the trader's losses are capped at $150 as the $850 profit from either contract will help reduce the loss of the $1000 investment capital.

The main danger of this strategy is when the expiration price is below $20 on the "Above" contract and higher than $25 for the "Below" contract since both contracts expire at different times (The "Below" contract is bought after the "Above" contract). In such a scenario, the trader will lose all his investment capital of $2000. In order to avoid such a scenario, the trader must ensure that his analysis is spot on. The fence trading strategy is a simple and good strategy to adopt when the conditions in the market are suitable for its implementation. Nevertheless, the strategy requires traders to have some decent background knowledge about the market in order for its successful implementation.

CHAPTER 6 FIBONACCI IN BINARY OPTIONS TRADING

Fibonacci Lines and Strike Price Locations

The Fibonacci retracement tool is one of the lesser used technical indicators in market analysis, but still forms

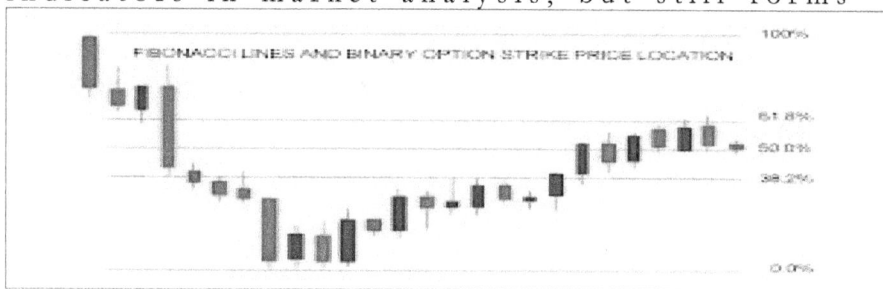

one of the best and most accurate strategies to accurately predict where prices are heading to.

Retracements are a regular part of trading. They happen all the time which means a trader needs to know how to use retracements to their advantage. This is where the Fibonacci retracement tool comes into play. The tool plots 5 horizontal lines on the charts which relate to 5 possible areas in which the price might retrace. The distances are expressed in terms of the percentage of the original move:
- 100%
- 61.8%
- 50%
- 38.2%
- 23.6%
- 0%

The Fibonacci sequence is essentially made up of a series of numbers where the 3rd number is the sum of the two numbers preceding it. An example is 0, 1, 1, 2, 3, 5, 8, 13, 21, and so on. It can be seen from the five levels above, the 23.6% and 38.2% levels are combined to provide the

61.8% standard. Once the charting tool is used with a pricing movement, these ratios stay true over any timeframe, providing high probability indicators into the areas where future levels of support and resistance might occur.

Once the price of the asset starts to indicate settling down, it is possible to see these as the levels where the prices will begin to show signs of stability.

Fibonacci retracements are at its best once the trader considers the trends in the market for an elongated time period. This might be difficult for the options with

shorter times of expiry, but binary options trading now can involve month long options offered by many platforms.

Fibonacci ratios have proven to be a very useful tool for assessing the barrier points in binary options. However, as with any other indicator system, they are not flawless despite being more accurate than others. They can be an indicator of where traders are probably to act, but as with most forms of investment extra verification from other indicators would provide a more accurate guide to the interpretation of price action and increase the ability to correctly forecast future price directions. There are a number of varieties of free charting packages which will provide this information just a couple of clicks of the mouse away.

Overall, using Fibonacci in binary options is suitable ideally only when looking at the shorter term and is not best used for the longer term. They can be one of the most accurate and popular strategies to assist the trader in the shorter term where asset prices are moving towards.

CHAPTER 7 STRADDLE STRATEGY

The straddle is a good trading strategy to adopt if you as an investor believe that the price of an underlying asset will fluctuate significantly but are unsure as to the
 direction of the fluctuation. For the straddle to be a profitable strategy, several conditions must be fulfilled first:
The price fluctuations must occur within a short term period.
The price swings must be significantly large.
There is an increase in implied volatility in the market.
If the price swings are not sufficiently large enough, then the profit earned might not be large enough to cover the premium paid for the options.
How to Profit From the Straddle Trading Strategy
For example, let us assume that you bought an EUR/USD 1.25 cent straddle for 4 cents expiring in a month time. If the EUR/USD rises to 1.35 cents, you would have gained 25 cents. Your total cost for the straddle is 4 cents for both the call and put (2 cents each). Because of the significantly large move in the price of the EUR/USD, you still have a net profit of 6 cents (10 cents – 4 cents = 6 cents).

Delta Hedging

Another way of profiting from the straddle is with "Delta Hedging". With Delta hedging, you reduce the risk linked to the price fluctuations of the underlying asset by equalizing your long and short market position. The investor risk exposure is zero with the delta hedge as he will not lose anything whether the market moves up or down. The only thing that he risks losing is the premium paid for the options.

Using the same example above, supposing the EUR/USD move from $1.25 to $1.30 and then back to $1.25. Let's suppose this fluctuation is repeated twice during the one month period which you own the straddle. When the EUR/USD price reached $1.30, it is possible to delta hedge at $1.30 with the anticipation that the market will continue to move. As the market move up, you become longer on the call and vice versa on the put. To remove this risk, you need to short the market and hence removing the delta. If the fluctuation occurs twice, you will be able to reap a profit from the price increase of $1.25 to $1.30 twice and $1.30 to $1.25 twice giving you a total profit of 20 cents on the delta hedge. This gain is more than sufficient to cover the losses that you incurred on the premiums.

Implied Volatility

An increase in the implied volatility of the market is another which you could gain from the straddle. The value of an option is determined by the implied volatility of the market. With an increase in the implied volatility of the market, the value of the option will naturally increase.

CHAPTER 8 DRAW DOWN STRATEGY

Draw Down is for intermediate and advanced traders and is a key concept

A draw down happens when a trader's investment capital is reduced after a streak of losing trades. It is measured by the difference between the peak of one's invested capital (equity capital) to that of a trough in one's invested capital.

Implication of Draw Down for Traders

As binary options traders, we are always looking for that extra edge to get us ahead in our trading. To do so, we develop trading systems to achieve this aim. So if we managed to develop a system which 70% profitable, theoretically this would mean that for every 100 trades, we would come out ahead 70 times. However, in the real world, things are not as clear-cut. Who is to say that we won't lose 30 times in a row before we start winning? This leaves us with an important question to think about. "Would we still be in the game after the 30th time of losing trades?"

Draw Downs are an intrinsic part of financial trading. This is the reason why we have to carefully manage our investment funds in order to be able to pull ourselves through a losing streak. Furthermore, each time a drawdown happens, we need to make more in terms of percentage to recuperate what we lost initially.

In the above example used earlier above, we lost 50% of our initial trading balance. Why?

We initially started off with $100,000. After a 50% draw down, we are left with $50,000. This mean to make back what we lost, we need to make $50,000 which is now 100% of our remaining investment capital. If we had stuck to the idea of recuperating just 50% back, we would have only recuperated $25,000. Add this amount to our remaining capital of $50,000 gives us only a total of $75,000, a net loss of 25% actually.

The table below summarizes what percentage return is needed to recover funds lost after a draw down:

Percentage Loss

Percentage required after Draw Down

- 10%
  - 11%
  - 20%
  - 25%
  - 30%
  - 43%
  - 40%
  - 67%
  - 50%
  - 100%
  - 60%
  - 150%
  - 70%
  - 233%
  - 80%
  - 400%
  - 90%
  - 900%

This is why it is important for traders to have good money management skills to limit their drawdowns and balance their risk-reward ratio to what is prudent and acceptable.

Causes of Draw Downs

One reason for draw downs is because of losing streaks which cause a trader suffers one loss after another. Another more significant reason for draw downs is because of a large winning market position reversing and breaking its trend. Successful trend trading strategy calls for a trader to continue trading until it breaks. Normally when a trend starts to break out, the trader will start adding to his market position until towards the end he becomes heavily invested. This is great if the trend continues but as we all know, all trends will eventually start to reverse. It is at this point of time that the trader will suffer considerable draw downs if he is not prepared for this eventuality.

Trading To Minimize The Impact Of Draw Downs

One strategy which traders can adopt to help them minimize the impact of draw downs is to adopt which is known as "Reverse Pyramiding". As opposed to "Standard Pyramiding" which calls for the trader to keep adding to a market position while it shows strength, reverse pyramiding calls for unwinding one's market position after a strong run. So if you are riding on a trend and becomes heavily invested in that trend, you should start to divest your market position once the market starts to pull back.

For example:

Supposing your portfolio had dropped by 5% since its peak, you start to scale back your portfolio by 25%. With reference to our example used above, if the peak of your portfolio was $100,000 and it had dropped to

$95,000 (5% draw down), you should start to reduce your portfolio to around $71,250 (25% of $95,000). For every 5% drop in the value of your portfolio, you would continue to reduce your holdings by a quarter.

If you continue to reverse pyramiding in this manner, you will find that the maximum drawdown that you will experience is 20% as you liquidated your holdings by 25% each time a 5% draw down is experienced. With this strategy, as your holdings become smaller, it gets harder and harder for your portfolio to be significantly affected. in fact, it would be next to impossible to touch the maximum 20% draw down as you would have exited most of your market position. Reverse pyramiding is a very simple tool to use but it is also extremely effective in helping traders minimizing their drawdowns while maximizing their profit potential

CHAPTER 9 COLLAR STRATEGY OPTIONS

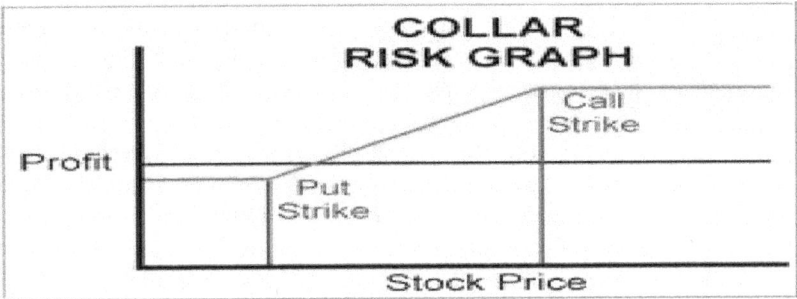

In the trading of financial instruments, you will always run the risk of losses whenever the market does not react or perform as anticipated. To help you minimize this risk, you can use a trading strategy commonly known as a "collar strategy". It involves reversing your risk by purchasing a call option and selling a put option or purchasing a put option and selling a call option.

As mentioned earlier, a collar trading strategy is used when you want to recuperate some of the transactional costs of a purchased option. This can be done by taking a market position in the opposite direction, i.e. selling an option. The attractive part of this strategy is that in certain situations, it is possible to completely offset price that you paid for the option resulting in what is known as a "costless collar". For example, let say you purchased a call option for a premium of $1.75. For this scenario to be a costless collar, you will need to sell a put option (for the same trading period) that has a price of $1.75 in order to totally offset the premium ($1.75) paid for the call option that you purchased earlier.

You normally use the collar trading strategy when you are unsure of the underlying price fluctuations. It is, in essence, a multi-legged protective trading strategy. What the collar does is to lock you into a protected price range. Downside protection comes into play when the strike price of the underlying asset falls below the strike price of the put option. However, you will forfeit any profit that is above the call option strike price.

As mentioned earlier, the collar trading strategy is a multi-legged trading strategy. Nevertheless, it can also be applied a single leg at a time. Earlier on, we also mentioned that it was possible for a collar to be costless, a situation where the money received from selling calls equal the premium paid for the puts. However, collars can also be structured in such a way that you can receive a premium or pay out some premium. The reason for structuring a collar that pays out some premium is due to the fact that you get to minimize your risks further by being able to liquidate an option that is further out of the money.

To illustrate this concept better, let's look at an example below:

Let's us assume that ABC Corporation is trading at $79. You purchased an ABC $88 call option with a bid price of $1.75. Supposed you simultaneously sold an ABC $88 put option also for $1.75. In this case, your collar will be a costless collar ($1.75 Call option bid price – $1.75 Put option bid price).

If we expand the above example further, you will end up paying some premium out if you had sold an ABC $85 put as the bid price would naturally be lower than $1.75. Let's assume the bid price for the $85 put is $1.24, this would mean that you will be paying out a premium of $0.51 ($1.75 Call option bid price – $1.24 Put option bid price). The end result of this collar is to allow you further room to maneuver until $78 instead of $88 as in the first instance.

It is always beneficial for a trader to trade using the collar strategy. As an investor, you will get to reduce the risk that is intrinsic in a volatile market with the collar. At the same time, you also benefit from not having to fork out a substantial sum for the benefit of mitigating the adverse effects of a volatile market. Although the collar is an interesting trading strategy, you need to have a robust understanding of how the market works before you can start applying as part of your trading strategy.

CHAPTER 10 PROTECTIVE PUT STRATEGY

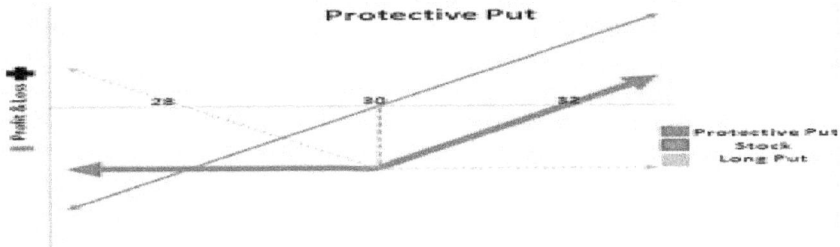

The Protective Put Strategy is for Advanced traders

Now let's learn how to use the protective put strategy. For those who are new to options, a "Put" option is a contract which gives the holder of the option the right to sell an underlying asset at a specific price within a specific time frame. It, however, does not impose any obligation on the holder of the option if he decided not to exercise the right.

Unlike a put buying strategy where the investor is selling short in the market, a protective put strategy is a strategy used by investors to minimize their risk profile

How the Strategy Works

As mentioned earlier, a put option allows an investor to sell an underlying asset at a predetermined strike price in exchange for the premium paid for the put option. For example, by purchasing an August 500 Gold put option for a premium of $1000, this entitles you to sell a gold futures contract at 500 per ounce on or before its expiration date in August.

With a protective put strategy, your risk is limited to the premium that you paid for the put option which in our example used is $1000. What differentiates a protective put strategy from a put buying strategy is the fact that the investor is buying the put option for the underlying asset which he already owns. The strategy is used to protect an investor's accumulated profit rather than his investment capital.

A Protective Put Strategy Example:

Let us assume that you own 100 shares of ABC stock bought at $50 per share. Ignoring commissions paid, your stock portfolio would require an investment of $5000 ($50 x 100 shares). Let's further assume that 3 months later the price of ABC stock has risen to $85 per share. This would translate into an unrealized profit of $3500 ($8500 − $5000).

Normally to lock in your profit, you would have to liquidate your portfolio. The main disadvantage of doing this is that it prevents you from reaping further gains should the stock prices increase further.

With a protective put strategy, you can overcome the dilemma of having to liquidate your stock portfolio. Your profits are locked in as you acquired the right to sell your stock at $85 with the put option you purchased. In return for this insurance, you pay a small premium for the put option. So your total risk is just limited to the premium paid for the put option.

The philosophy behind the protective put strategy differs from the covered call strategy in two main ways. First, the protective put strategy calls for you as the investor to purchase the put option for a premium. The covered call strategy calls for you to sell a call option to receive a premium. Second, the protective put strategy is more suited to markets which are high volatile. The covered call strategy is geared more towards the market with relatively low volatility. As mentioned earlier, the main goal of the protective put strategy is risk mitigation for an underlying asset or portfolio thus it is not surprising to sometimes find investors combining the use of this strategy with the covered call strategy.

CHAPTER 11 COVERED CALL STRATEGY

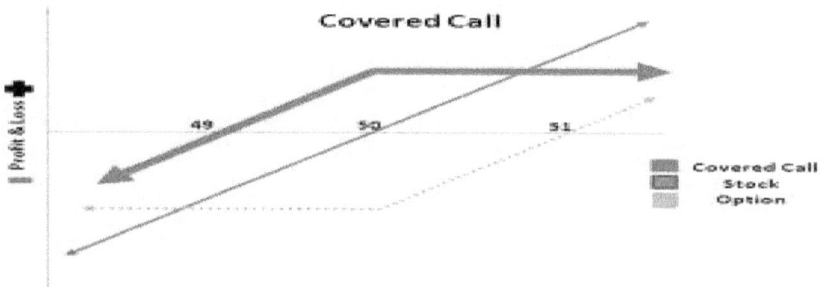

One of the ways which you can reduce your trading risk is to employ the use of the covered call strategy. The strategy is specifically used is a situation when you are holding a long market position in an asset. In order to reduce the risk in this situation, you can write (sell) a call option on that asset. The idea of this is to generate additional income (option's premium) from the asset traded by selling the option later. An incidental benefit of this strategy is that you also get to minimize the extent of your losses if the market suddenly tanked

Call Options Defined

In order to fully understand the concept of the Covered call strategy, it is important to have some basic knowledge about what options are. Options are essentially financial contracts that give the holder of the option the right to buy or sell a particular asset at a specific strike price on or before the date which the option will expire. It should be noted that the option does not oblige the holder to exercise these rights.

With a Call Option, the holder of the option gets to buy an asset at the stated strike price on or before its expiry. Let's say that you strongly believe that the

USD/JPY trading at 98.20 will rise higher in the short term. You can benefit from this rise by purchasing a near term USD/JPY Call Option that allows you to buy the USD/JPY at the current rate of 98.20. In the event the USD/JPY does rise higher to say 115.00, exercising the call option will allow you to profit from the exchange rate differential, in this case, 16.8 yen (115.00 -98.20). Supposing the anticipated rise in the USD/JPY did not occur, in this case, you can choose not to exercise the call option. Your loss will then be just limited to the premium that you paid for the near term USD/JPY Call option.

Naked Call Vs Covered Call

In the above example, we discussed how call options work. On the other side of the equation, there is also the seller of the option who assumes the unlimited risk. Thus when you as an investor become an option seller, you will actually be assuming an unlimited level of risk especially in "naked call" scenarios. A "naked call" is defined as a situation where an option seller sells an option without owning the underlying asset for the option.

In order to mitigate the risk level, the covered call strategy can be employed. In essence, a covered call strategy requires the option seller to own the underlying asset so the call option is backed or covered by actual ownership of the asset. Thus, in the event the market moves against you and the call option get exercised, you are hedged against unlimited losses.

At this stage, you might be wondering why to bother dealing with covered call options and not just deal in the underlying asset only. Well, the thing is with covered call options, even if the option that you sold get exercised forcing you to sell the underlying asset at the strike price, you will still get to earn the premium from the option sold.

For example, let's say you own several lots of USD/JPY. You decided to sell call options for the USD/JPY for a premium of 50 cents with a strike price of 110.00 while it is still trading at 98.00. So if the USD/JPY doesn't move beyond 110.00, you will have earned the premium of 50 cents from the options sold. However, if the USD/JPY moves beyond 110.00 (the strike price), then you will be forced to sell the USD/JPY at 110.00 to the holder of the call options. As you can see in this scenario, the risk is mitigated as you already owned USD/JPY and you also get to earn additional income (premium) from the options sold.

Although the covered call strategy can be quite a complex strategy, nevertheless it is a good strategy to employ when you want to:

Earn a premium from selling a call to assume the obligation of selling an underlying asset at a specified price.

Take profit only at a level which is above the current price level.

Forsake the upside profit potential in return for some downside protection.

CHAPTER 12 A GREAT BINARY OPTIONS STRATEGY LONG BOX TRADING

To become a successful binary options trader, one doesn't need to be a rocket scientist. All it takes is some basic mathematical skills and a mind that is capable of making straightforward analysis. For the Long Box trading strategy, a trader will be concerned about buying simultaneous purchase and selling of a call and put options with identical strike prices and expiration times respectively. The strategy is normally adopted by traders when the options are underpriced in comparison to their expiration values. In other words, the trader can lock in profit immediately if the premiums paid for the call and put options is substantially lower than the combined expiration value of the options.

Although the long box strategy may sound complex initially, it is in essence no different from many other trading strategies which a trader may employ during the course of his trading. The basic essence of all trading activities calls for the buying and selling options until a trader's profit level reaches to a certain level of the expiration value. To sum it up, the long box trading strategy is about:
- Higher Strike Price – Lower Strike Price = Expiration Value of Box
- Expiration Value of Box – Net Premium Paid = Risk-free Profit
- The Benefits Of The Long Box Trading Strategy
- Ability to convert overpriced options to profits
- No fear in implementing this strategy as it is risk-free.
- Earn instant risk-free profit even though the gain might not be huge.

Disadvantages Of The Strategy

Must be vigilant with regards to the premiums and possible payout.
Need to perform a market analysis to look for overpriced options.
Traders cannot hope for a large gain.

As the possible gains from the long box strategy will not be large, traders need to bear in mind that all their gains could be wiped out if their broker charges a high spread. This obviously isn't so relevant with binaries as the trader is not usually charged a spread in any case.Hence, a trader cannot afford to let his guard anytime while he is using this strategy.

CHAPTER 13 MONEY MANAGEMENT-STOP LOSS AND PROFIT TAKING

Stop Loss and Profit Taking is for the intermediate and advanced traders

Before beginning to trade in the financial markets, you must have your money management strategy sorted out first. This involves allocating sufficient trading capital and deciding how much money that you are willing to lose. You also need to devise a proper trading strategy that allows for a realistic risk to reward ratio using stop loss techniques and take profit.

Ideally, the risk to reward ratio should be one where the profit level is at least three times that of the amount you risk. That mean to earn $3, the maximum that you should risk is only $1. Mathematical speaking, with a 3 to 1 ratio, you will need to have a trading strategy that will win more than 25% of the time.

For example:

Let say out of 8 trades, we win 2 times (2 x $3 = $6) and lose 6 trades (6 x $1 = $6). This mean our profits will be canceled by our losses. So in order to have any gains, we need a trading strategy that will allow us to win more than a quarter of the time.

Never ignore this important trading philosophy about balancing your risk to reward ratio. If you do so, you will just end up losing money in the long run.

Stop Loss As Part Of The Risk Management Strategy

As part of your risk management strategy, you need to consider how much that you are willing to risk based on your allocated investment capital. This translates into how much market swing that you are willing to accept against your market position. Once you have decided on this, you will able to use an important tool for risk management, the stop loss order.

The stop loss order lets a trader stop out of a trade when prices reached a predetermined level. It can be based on a percentage move in market prices or potential dollar amount of money lost.

There are several ways of determining where to place the stop loss order. It can be based on historical movements of prices, technical analysis or just purely on a theoretical dollar amount of losses that you can bear.

With strategies based on historical movements of prices, traders have the advantage of backtesting a range of stop loss amounts to see which the best stop loss level is for them.

Technical analysis also provides a very reliable way of determining a stop loss level. Used in conjunction with trendlines, support and resistance lines provide a good graphical illustration on where a stop loss level could be placed.

From the chart illustrated below, the investor here has decided to place his stop loss at the recent low to protect his profit level.

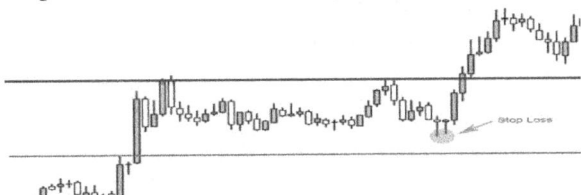

Beside from support and resistance levels, there are also other indicators like trend lines, moving averages which a trader can employ to help him decide where to place his stop loss.

Another important aspect of stop loss is that it can be dynamic. This mean an investor can set his stop loss in accordance with a percentage movement in the market. This type of stop loss is known as a trailing stop loss.

Profit Taking

Equally important for a trader is knowing when to exit a trade. This determination should be made beforehand just like the determination on how much to risk. Just like the way you determine your risk level, profit taking can be based on a theoretical dollar amount, as a percent of market movements or purely based on a level determined through technical analysis. Using the support and resistance lines is an excellent way of determining your profit level.

Regardless of the profit level, you should always make this determination in conjunction with the amount of money that you are willing to lose. Always avoid placing trades where your risk reward ratio is negative.

CHAPTER 14 RISK AND BET SIZE-HEDGING AND STOP LOSS

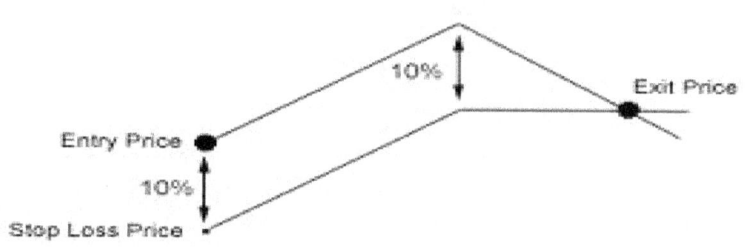

Manage Your Risk with Trailing Stop Loss

Trailing stop loss is used by investors to ensure that their risk to reward profile remains the same even after the market has moved higher. Compared to the fixed stop loss, the trailing stop offers one key advantage. It continues to protect an investor's trading capital even when the market drops. At the same time, because of is trailing feature, the investor is able to maximize his profit potential without having to sacrifice his risk protection level.

To understand the concept better, let us assume that the trailing stop loss is fixed at 5% of the amount invested or at a fixed spread of 20 cents. Regardless of whether it is a fixed percentage or at a fixed spread amount, the trailing stop is tied to the trading day's high by the predetermined ratio or amount. The crucial thing to note is that once the trailing stop level is set, it doesn't drop backward. For example, if the price happens to drop lower than the trailing stop value, it will trigger the stop loss.

One good thing about the trailing stop loss is that it helps to remove the emotional aspect of trading. The trailing stop loss value is usually set at the optimal level because the decision is usually arrived at after a calm and focused analysis of the information presented by the trading charts. There is no second guessing here. Nevertheless, there is the danger of setting the trailing stop too tightly that it is easily triggered by minor price drops causing investors to fret over "lost" profits.

Bet Size

Apart from mitigating your possible losses and maximizing your profit potentials with stop losses and take profit levels, you also need to consider your bet size in your trading strategy. The main idea of doing this is to preserve your trading capital so you can survive the rigors of the market to be able to trade the next day. Every experienced trader knows that returns commensurate with risk. The higher the risk level, the higher the returns. However, there is a thin line between trading for maximum profitability to trading with greed. As the famous Wall Street saying goes, "Bulls make money, bears make money, pigs get slaughtered".

The question is how much capital should be risked in a trade? If we risked too little, our return would hardly be significant to make any dent in our ending balance. If we risked a large amount, we run the risk of incurring a large loss which could possibly deplete our investment capital.

To help traders determine the appropriate amount to invest, they have relied upon several mathematical models to help them deal with the impasse between risk and return.

The Monte Carlo Simulation model uses historical back-testing to see what the optimal bet size is. The Kelly formula, on the other hand, assigns fixed ratios of capital to be invested in each trade based on their long-term capital growth. The Fixed Ratio method discussed by Ryan Jones in his book "The Trading Game" tries to balance geometric growth against risk. This method tries to mitigate the risk level by adjusting the trade size downward.

The fact is there is no foolproof money management model. Each of the mathematical models mentioned above suffers from limitations in one form or another. The models are not able to fully integrate the risk element into their calculations. For methods that placed a secondary importance on the relationship between risk and capital losses, they run the risk of making traders complacent about the degree of risks involved in trading.

At the end of the day, it doesn't really matter if the strategy used is systematic or discretionary one. What is more important for you as a trader is to create a trading strategy which allows you to manage your investment capital in a distinct manner. This is one of the keystone foundations in ensuring that your trading strategy is a successful one.

You have to remember that the end goal is to ensure that your investment capital remains relatively intact. You want to be able to place trades over a period of time and not have your trading career cut short due to massive draw downs. Finding the optimal bet size is not an easy task but your trading strategy must be flexible enough to allow you to determine your "Uncle Point", that is the point where you find out if your trading strategy really works or not.

Managing Your Portfolio

Referred to as an art as well as a science, portfolio management involves the delicate task of balancing the risk undertaken to maintain the portfolio to maximizing its return. This includes having a range of diversified investment to help reduce the risk involved. As an investor, you do not want to get into a situation where you hold several market positions which are highly correlated. Having highly correlated investments mean an adverse move in one position could affect all the correlated investments. In short, you are essentially just holding a large single position which has the potential of suffering a large draw down.

Portfolio Hedging

Portfolio hedging in the process in which investors use a variety of strategies to help them reduce their portfolio risk exposure to negative directional movements in the market.

How Portfolio Hedging Work?

To hedge your portfolio, you need to use financial derivatives like options and futures to help you curb your losses. For example, if you are concerned about the short-term price fluctuations that can affect your investment, you can purchase put options to offset your losses with the profits from the put options. There are a large variety of options and futures that investors can use to hedge against price swings in stocks, commodities, currency pairs and changes in the interest rate.

As mentioned earlier, the end goal of hedging your portfolio is to curb against potential losses. This insurance, however, comes with a price because by hedging you also limit a number of potential profits that you could earn. Thus, it falls down to you as an investor to weigh the cost of hedging against the benefit that you might get in return.

CHAPTER 15 SCALPING: BINARY OPTIONS TRADING

Scalping: Binary Options Strategies

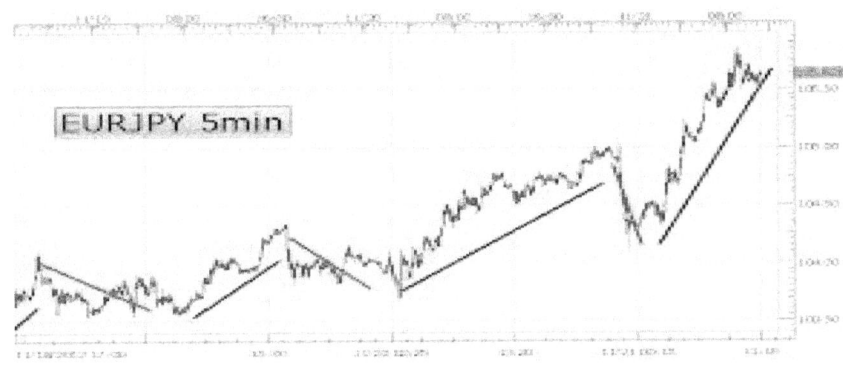

In Cowboy movies, the word scalping holds a sinister meaning but in the world of online financial trading, it is a trading technique used by traders to skim profits from the financial markets. The main idea behind this trading technique is for traders to open a market position and close it within minutes once they have picked up just a few pips in profit. If we were to draw an analogy to this form of trading then it would be filling a bucket up by drip feeding. Because of their success rate traders can make thousands albeit at a slow rate, while many brokers tend to dislike scalpers. Although scalping is normally done by Forex traders, the same trading technique can also be employed in binary options trading.

Scalping with binary options is actually quite similar to scalping in Forex trading. The only main difference is that with binary options, the positions are closed automatically due to the expiry of the contract. Whereas scalping in Forex trading requires that the trader closes the market position.

Time Frame for Scalping

To scalp with binary options, traders need to use options with a short expiry time. Hence, the best options to employ for scalping would 60-

second options. Although more and more binary options brokers are offering 60-second options trades, it should be borne in mind that not all brokers offer this type of trade. So check first if your broker offers this type of trade. Nevertheless, when 60-second options are not available, 15 minutes and 30 minutes binary options can also be

utilized. Another way to scalp is by using Option Builder trades since Option Builder allows traders to determine the expiry time. Banc de Binary and Trader XP both offer the Option Builder platform

Tools for Scalping

Once you have decided on the time frame that you want to trade in, the next step is to determine the tools that you need before deciding to open a market position. Normally, the tools employed by scalpers include candlestick charts, price action analysis and technical indicators. Chart patterns analysis is not suitable as the analysis might yield the wrong analysis due to the longer time frame required. Only charts with a minimum time frame of 1 minute and a maximum of 15 minutes should be used if you want to employ scalping trading techniques. The main reason for this is so any information obtained from your analysis of the charts stays relevant. You don't want to analyze a 6-hour chart for a trade that is going to play out in just 60 seconds.

It all sounds pretty easy but remember that scalping is highly speculative. Practice often and be sure that you know what you are doing before you decide to start scalping! It's a fact that inexperienced traders end up with more losses than wins.

CHAPTER 16 THE FOREX MULTIPLE TIME FRAMES STRATEGY WITH BINARY OPTION

For this trading strategy, you will need a decent charting software and some patience.

Although trading with multiple time frames is not a new concept among traders in the forex circle, it is relatively unheard-of among binary options traders. Because binary options are normally traded with a relatively short time period, many traders choose to disregard multiple time frames trading. They think this trading system is not suitable for short-term instruments like binary options. However, losing sight of the bigger picture can often result in missing clear signals for probable market entry points.

Multiple Time Frames Trading System Explained

The multiple time frames trading system requires the monitoring of an asset's price movements across different time frames. Although there is no hard and fast rule regarding the number of the time frame required in this trading system, there are still guidelines that should be followed. Usually, three different time frames should suffice for a broad overview of the market. Using less than three-time frames will result in insufficient data for an inconclusive analysis while excessive time frames will only result in redundant analysis. When selecting the time frames to use, it is important to bear in mind "The Rule Of Four".

Medium Term Time Frame

The first stage of choosing your time frame is to select a medium term time frame which is representative of how long you hold your trade. So if you normally hold your trades for 6 hours (360 minutes), then that should be the time frame you use for your medium-term time frame.

Short Term and Long Term Time Frames

Bearing in mind the "Rule of four", your short term time frame should be 90 minutes (360 mins/ 4) while your long term time frame should be 24 hours (360 mins x 4). By following this basic guideline, we can see how we bring relevancy in our selection of time frames. Clearly, if you are holding a trade for around 6 hours at a time, there is no point having a 15 minute short term time frame chart. Otherwise, you will end up with 24 segments of 15 minutes chart to constantly review. The same reasoning goes for long term time frame selection.

Putting Theory To Work

In a multiple time frame trading situation, it is always best to do your analysis on a top-down basis. Hence, you will start your analysis on the long term time frame first and then work your way down to the medium term time frame and short term time frame respectively.

Long Time Term Frame

By looking at the long-term time frame, you can see the direction where the general trend is heading toward to. At this point, it is still too early to execute a trade. What should be noted is that when you do make your trade after all the analysis, it should be in the same direction as the general trend.

Medium Term Time Frame

As you focus more closely on the medium timeframe, spikes within the general trend will start to become more visible. The medium time frame is the most flexible frequencies among all the three-time frames as it is possible to get a sense of the short term and long term frames with it. Actually, it is also the time frame which most traders relied upon when planning their trades.

Short Term Time Frame

Your trades should only be concluded on this time frame. As you narrow down your focus to shorter time frames, you will notice that smaller price movements which are not so obvious before will become clearer. This will enable you to pick a vantage point to enter the market in the same direction of the general trend defined by the longer time frames.

When you combine all the analysis from the three-time frames, you will definitely improve the odds for a successful trade. A top down approach helps a trader to trade smartly in sync with the market trend. Poor trades due to temporary market fluctuations can be avoided entirely when trades are planned ahead in a progressive manner.

CHAPTER 17 IDENTIFYING TREND REVERSALS

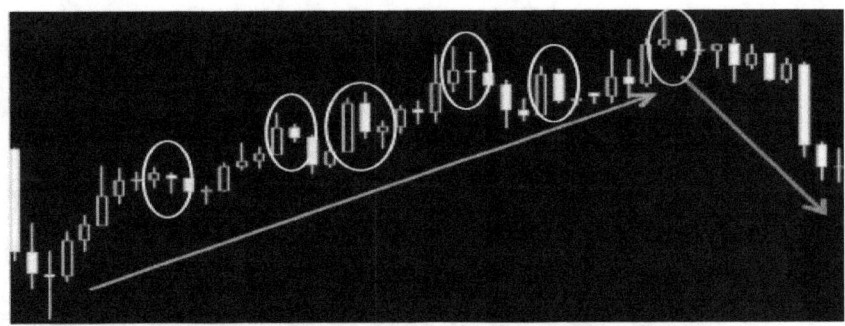

The trend is your friend is an oft-repeated maxim of trading, and a lot of binary options trading strategies hinge around identifying a trend and trading with it. Of course, every market is volatile, and every trend comes to an end. So, what do you do when the trend ends?

Knowing when to get into the market is an essential skill, but getting out at the right time is just as important. With binary options, it's a little easier to know when to get out, because they expire at a fixed time. But, if you are following a trend, how do you know if it's going to last until the option expires, and how do you know whether it's a good idea to get into another option right after, taking advantage of the continuing trend?

Let's take the following chart:

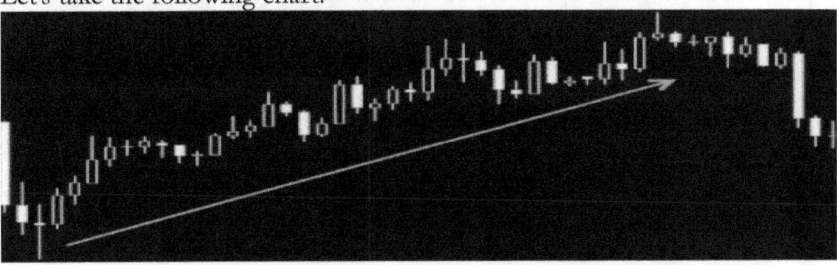

It shows a clearly defined rising trend. However, it didn't just go up and up but came across different pauses lung the way when it went down for a brief bit. These are corrections, and they happen in every market. The trouble is identifying when a change in direction is just a correction, or it's an outright reversal as we see at the end of the chart. This is even more important in binary options, because if you've identified the upwards trend, you don't want to get caught in one of those corrections.

Of course, there is no way of predicting the future, but there is a host of tools that investors can use to identify patterns that give an indication of when a reversal is imminent. A lot of them use sophisticated indicators like Bollinger bands, Commodity Channel and Relative Strength indices, and the more exotic Ichimoku clouds.

But you can get a leg up by just looking at the graph.

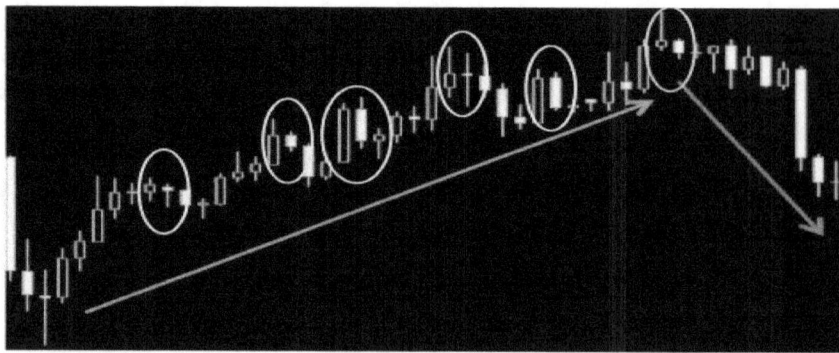

The movements on the graph can give you an idea of how strong a movement is, and often an indication of when a trend is starting to get exhausted. One of the more common indicators that an asset is in the process of reversing is that its downward movements become stronger than its upward movements.

This is a pattern called "engulfing"; either a "bullish engulfing" meaning the equity is about to start to go up, or a "bearish engulfing" meaning it will go down. They are the easiest to identify with candle or bar graphs, although you can spot them in a line graph with a very keen eye. Let's go back to the graph: Notice at each time the asset started a correction, the downward candle (bear candle) was shorter than the upward candle that preceded it (in other words, it went down less than it went up in identical time periods).

But later, when the trend reverses, the downward candle is longer than the preceding one, indicating that the downward movement is stronger. It's important to remember that this doesn't happen every time, but it can give you an edge in predicting when the market will turn around. This will allow you to prevent getting in on the wrong side of the trend, or be able to catch on to the new trend quickly.

CONCLUSION

Which Type of Binary Options Trader Are You?

Hey, Binary Options Traders, ask yourself this:

Binary options traders uncle samKnowing the kind of trader that you also help in the developing of your trading plan. So ask yourself which one of the following best suits your trading type:

A Day trader

Day traders only trade within the trading day with no overnight positions. Selections of trades are normally done at the start of the trading day. Most binary options traders fall under this category.

A Position Trader

Position Traders are longer term traders with trades spanning over weeks or months. Fundamental analysis plays a more important part here. If you are more comfortable in being a position trader, then binary options trading is not for you as it is fast moving with the trading period spanning several days at the most.

A Scalper

In contrast to position traders, scalpers' trades only last seconds or minutes. The main objective is to make as many trades as possible within the trading day. Here, volume rules over pips. This is the ideal category for binary options traders, especially those that trade using 60-second platforms.

A Swing Trader

Swing traders trades are normally over several days. Their trades are done with prior planning and then left to their own throughout the trading day. These traders normally do not have time to constant monitor their charts which why they adopt such a trading style.

Irrespective of your trading style, it is important that the style suits your lifestyle. Are you trying to make a second income? Perhaps trade over the weekends or is this your career?

Developing Your Own Trading Plan

Share this:Share via TwitterShare via LinkedInShare via FacebookShare via Google

Because of our individuality, we all have different attitudes, different experiences and different levels of tolerance to risk. By developing your own trading plan, you are cultivating one of the two main qualities that are needed from trading discipline. The other factor needed is being able to stick to your trading plan. With a rock solid discipline as your foundation, your goal as a successful trader is only a matter of time.

So What Is A Trading Plan?

A trading plan is a systematic way of executing your trade based on your market outlook and analysis after factoring in your personal psychology and appetite for risk. Always bear in mind that regardless of how well drafted your trading plan is, it is useless if you are unable to stick to it. It is only those who kept an iron clad disciplined approach towards trading survive the ups and downs of the market and still come out ahead. With a trading plan:

Trading is less chaotic as there is a roadmap to follow.

You have little stress as you are more in control of the situation.

You can monitor and track your performance and correct any shortcomings that you might have.

You will reduce the number of bad trades that you will make.

You can prevent any bad psychological bad habits from developing.

Trading outside the comfort zone is easy as you know what you are doing.

Any trading mistakes can be corrected quickly but things spiral out of control. Trading plans are developed to cater for various scenarios, best case, worse case and expected results.

A trading plan is dynamic. There is always room for improvements and adaptations. Nothing is set in stone. If the market situation reQuires you to adapt, then adjust your trading plan accordingly.

Keeping a Trading Journal

Date	Entry time	Entry price	Exit price	Contracts / Lot size	Market / Limit	Long / Short	Market	Which chart	Signal Type	brokerage	P/L	Notes
9am	1594	1596	1 contract	limit	L	ES	60min	bounce	$5	$95	Followed my plan

Total P/L $95

Keeping a Trading Journal is Crucial!

Although a tedious task, keeping a trading journal is crucial if you are aiming to be an effective trader. You need to be able to measure and keep track of your performance before you are able to improve and correct past mistakes. This is why having a proper journal is important.

Unless you have a photographic memory, it is impossible to remember all your trading details like reasons why you made a particular trade, why you selected a certain entry point or why you exited the market at a certain point. Even though you can refer to your trading or transaction logs provided by your broker, those data does not tell you the "reasons" for the trade. In other words, you cannot reflect back on your trading psychology.

For example:

Your trading plan calls for you to purchase the USD/JPY call options. However, your gut feeling tells you that this trade will not work and you are taking the trade because you are just sticking to your trading plan.

Later, halfway through the trade, you find that the market is starting to move against you and this sets you off thinking that why didn't you listen to your gut instinct in the first place. Prompted by the "demons" in your mind, you decided to close the trade early to minimize your losses.

Shortly after closing your trade, you find that the market has turned and is moving as expected according to your trading plan. The end result is that you could have turned a profit instead of suffering a loss. Without recording down the reason for the unplanned exit, you will never know that your emotion got the better of you here. With a written record in your trading journal, you will always be reminded that you must not let your emotion rule your trade.

Back Testing Your Binary Options Trading Strategies

Share this:Share via TwitterShare via LinkedInShare via FacebookShare via Google

Backtesting is where traders test their trading strategies using historical price data.

Instead of trading with new unproven trading strategies for the period ahead, a trader can use the relevant price data to simulate conditions to test the effectiveness of the newly developed strategy. The logic is if a trading strategy works well with historical data then it should also perform well in the future.

Backtesting is a critical part of trading system development as it is possible to structure rules on how the strategy should work using historical data. For example, you could base your strategy on an assumption that a specific asset tends to deviate away from its 20-period moving average by a few points away before sliding back to the moving average. With proper back testing, valuable information can be gained such as:

- Profit/Loss Levels
- Projected Returns
- Trading Success Ratio

The ultimate benefit that you will gain is confidence in the fact that your trading strategy is working properly before applying it in the real world.

Before back testing, it is important to get the correct mix of price actions and technical indicators so the test will yield results of significance. Another point to remember about backtesting is to test your strategy over a long term period rather than just over small short time periods. This is to avoid a phenomenon known as "over optimization" where the strategy only works for the short-term periods but not over a broader range of time periods.

I wish you the best in your trading.

www.ingramcontent.com/pod-product-compliance
Lightning Source LLC
Chambersburg PA
CBHW070405190526
45169CB00003B/1125